Guess What

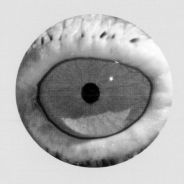

Published in the United States of America by
Cherry Lake Publishing
Ann Arbor, Michigan
www.cherrylakepublishing.com

Content Adviser: Susan Heinrichs Gray
Reading Adviser: Marla Conn, ReadAbility, Inc.
Book Design: Felicia Macheske

Photo Credits: © pandapawk/Shutterstock.com, cover; © James Laurie/Shutterstock.com, 1, 4; © maratr/Shutterstock.com, 3; val lawless/Shutterstock.com, 7; Vadim Petrakov/Shutterstock.com, 9; © kuponjabah/Shutterstock.com, 10; © Martin Spurny/Shutterstock.com, 13; © nattanan726/Shutterstock.com, 16; © Fuse/Thinkstock, 18; © cyo bo/Shutterstock.com, 21; © Eric Isselée/Shutterstock.com, back cover; © Andrey_Kuzmin/Shutterstock.com, back cover

Library of Congress Cataloging-in-Publication Data

Calhoun, Kelly, author.
 Poised and pink / Kelly Calhoun.
 pages cm. — (Guess what)
 Summary: "Young children are natural problem solvers and always looking for answers, especially when it involves animals. Guess What: Poised and Pink: Flamingo provides young curious readers with striking visual clues and simply written hints. Using the photos and text, readers rely on visual literacy skills, reading, and reasoning as they solve the animal mystery. Clearly written facts give readers a deeper understanding of how the animal lives. Additional text features, including a glossary and an index, help students locate information and learn new words."— Provided by publisher.
 Audience: Ages 5-8
 Audience: K to grade 3
 Includes index.
 ISBN 978-1-63362-625-6 (hardcover) — ISBN 978-1-63362-715-4 (pbk.) — ISBN 978-1-63362-805-2 (pdf) — ISBN 978-1-63362-895-3 (ebook)
 1. Flamingos—Juvenile literature. 2. Children's questions and answers. I. Title.

 QL696.C56C35 2016
 598.3'5—dc23

 2015003097

Cherry Lake Publishing would like to acknowledge the work of The Partnership for 21st Century Skills.
Please visit *www.p21.org* for more information.

Printed in the United States of America
Corporate Graphics Inc.

Table of Contents

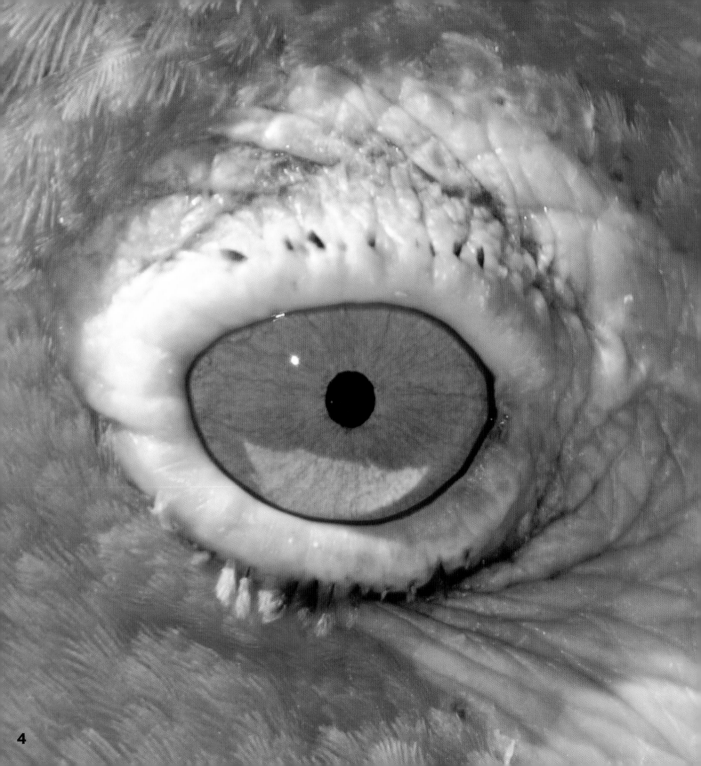

4

I like to keep an eye on my friends.

My body is covered with feathers.

I have
a long,
curving
neck.

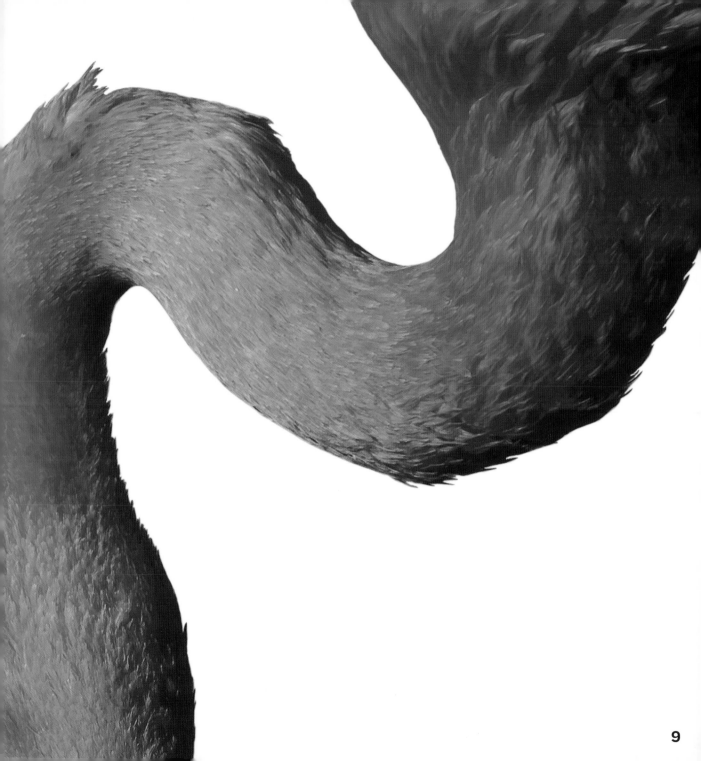

My webbed **feet** help me walk in the mud.

I have a large, curved beak.

I have very long, thin legs.

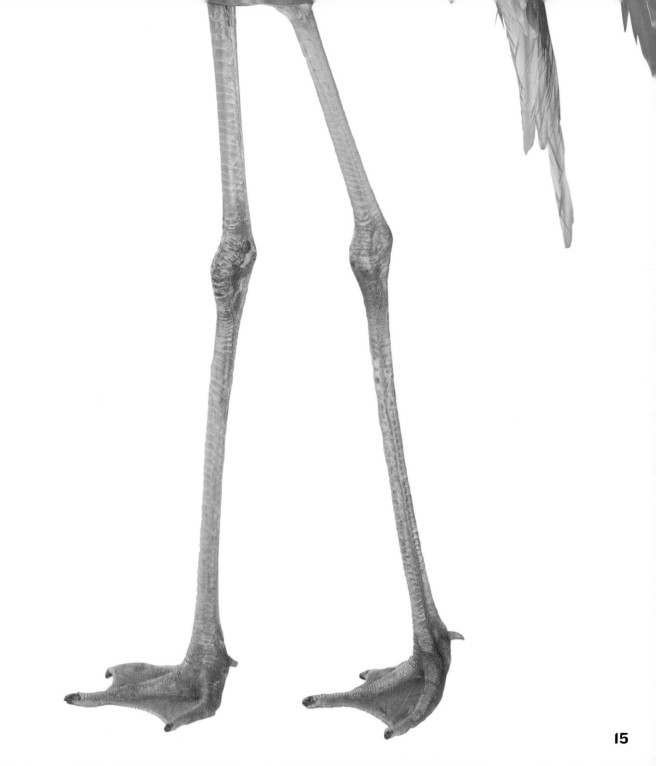

The food I eat can make me turn pink.

I fly in flocks with other birds like me.

Do you know what I am?

I'm a Flamingo!

About Flamingos

1. Flamingos have long, curving necks.

2. Flamingos often stand on one leg.

3. Flamingos like to stay in large groups.

4. Baby flamingos are white and gray, not pink.

5. Female flamingos lay only one egg per year.

Glossary

curving (KUR-veeng) bent, not straight

flocks (flakhs) groups of animals of one kind that live, travel, or feed together

groups (groops) numbers of things together that go together or have something in common

thin (thin) not fat; slender

webbed (webd) having an area of skin between the fingers or toes

Index